The Next-Door Noise

This book is dedicated to my wonderful parents,
Jane & Nigel Gray, who have always believed in me.

Copyright © 2023 Lucy Gray Moreland

All rights reserved. No part of this book may be reproduced or distributed in any form without prior written permission from the author, with the exception of non-commercial uses permitted by copyright law.

One quiet, happy morning, while I sat and played inside,
My Mummy looked outside and said to Daddy, "They've arrived!"

And then a giant thing began – it happened everywhere!
The room, my head, my tummy filled with noise and shock and scare!

"Noise!" I cried to Mummy - to tell her what I'd heard.
I scrambled up to cling and hug, and hide myself in her.

"Noise!" I cried to Mummy - to tell her what I felt,
"It's just Next-Door," she told me, as she cradled me and knelt.

RUMBLE, RUMBLE, WHINE and CRASH and NEE-OO and NEEE-OOR!
"Noise!" I cried to Mummy and she said, 'It's just Next-Door'.

She whispered things and held me tight but, still, I clung to Mummy
Because I cannot stand the Next-Door wobbles in my tummy!

What if it's a helicopter coming close to here?
Is the Next-Door Noise the sound it makes when it comes near?

I cannot find a way to sit and laugh, or play with toys,
Because I'm hating every moment of the Next-Door Noise.

Sometimes, it goes quiet, then I think it's gone away
But, next, an awful CRANKING sound shows that it's here to stay.

We went upstairs to have my nap but, as I touched my cot,
The **BASHING** starts - I cry and cry – oh please don't leave – do not!

We go back down, I cuddle up in Mummy's arms instead.
But there's no sleep for me today, with **SCREECHES** in in my head.

What if it's a Monster that is **STOMPING** up to me?
Is the Next-Door Monster hiding somewhere I can't see?

There is no napping to be done, and no sleep to be found,
Because it never ends – the never-ending, Next-Door sound!

And, when the time for lunch was here, I sat up in my chair.
My favourite salmon pasta was just in my bowl – right there!

But, when I go to hold my fork, the **KNOCKING** is too much!
I'm far too scared for eating food, it must remain untouched.

What if it's a tower of plates that someone's stacked too high?
Will the Next-Door plates come falling, **CRASHING** from the sky?

I cannot have my favourite salmon pasta, or my drink
Because I can't escape the Next-Door **BANG** and **SMASH** and **CLINK**!

When bath time came, I sank into the water, calm and warm.
I love to touch the bubbles when they burst and when they form.

But, as my little boat sets sail across the soapy waves,
The **SHOUTING** and the **BASHING** make me jump and stop my games.

What if it's a great big wave that's just about to fall?
Is the Next-Door Noise about to come right through the wall?

I cannot go into my bath to sit and play and splash!
Oh, will it ever stop? The Next-Door **CLOMP** and **CLAP** and **CLASH**!

At bedtime, Mummy put me down and Dad turned off the light.
"Noise?" I asked, and Mummy said, "There'll be no more tonight."

"Mummy promise," Mummy said, and so I know it's true.
It's been so long since sleeping that I yawn and sleep right through.

When light came through my window and the morning had arrived,
I sat up straight and listened for the scary noise outside.

And Mummy came and scooped me up with smiles, and eyes and arms
But **RUMBLE... RUMBLE...** it begins – I whimper in alarm.

Then Mummy got my coat and shoes and said, "We're going to see!"
But where is breakfast? Playtime first! Oh, why all this hurry?

Then out the door - the sound is loud... I've not gone here before.
We're going towards the house that's making all the Noise Next-Door.

I'm scared, I'm scared, what does this mean? Whatever will I see?
The helicopter, monster, plates, the great big wave, and me?

But, as we go around the house, I smile and clap my hands
At hammers, tools and drills and saws, and men and big white vans!

Their garden had machines the men brought with them when they came!
The men gave me high fives, and smiled, and waved, and said my name!

They let me see and touch the stuff which causes all the **BOOM**!
They even said there'll be a real digger coming soon!

When Mummy took me home, we waved goodbye, and I said, "Wow!"
I found I wasn't clinging quite so tightly to her now.

I skipped away from Mummy as we walked back through our door,
Because the Next-Door Noise was not so scary anymore.

And now, at play or bath time, having dinner or my nap,
Although I hear the scary **SCRATCH** and **WHIZZ** and **CRASH** and **TAP**,

I know it's the exciting things I felt and touched and saw.
'Noise...' I think - but then I say, 'I know... it's just Next-Door!'

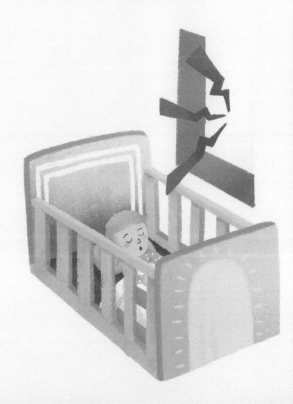

The End

About The Author

Lucy Moreland is a children's author and primary school teacher, living in Walton-on-Thames, Surrey. She is a mother and enjoys using the everyday experiences of her son to inspire her writing. The Next-Door Noise is based on the real-life experience of her two-year-old son, who felt terrified when some building work was taking place in her neighbours' house.

To the neighbours – in all honesty – thank you for the Noise! I couldn't have written this without you!

Other publications by Lucy include the Phone-Away Day, a story about a family who decides to put their screens away for a day, and have some wholesome family fun. You can find it in Kindle and paperback formats here: